Planet Hunting

by
David Orme

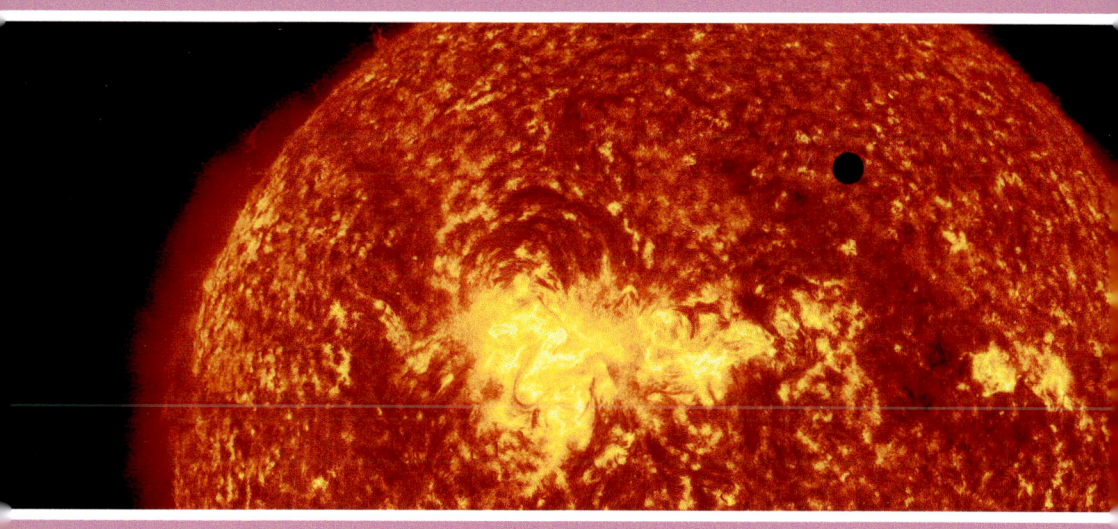

Thunderbolts

Planet Hunting
by David Orme

Illustrated by Dan Chernett

Published by Ransom Publishing Ltd.
Unit 7 Brocklands Farm, West Meon, Hants. GU32 1JN, UK
www.ransom.co.uk

ISBN   978 178127 074 5

First published in 2013
Reprinted 2021, 2023

Copyright © 2013 Ransom Publishing Ltd.

Illustrations copyright © 2013 Dan Chernett
'Get the Facts' section - images copyright: cover, prelims, passim – European Southern Observatory, NASA/Ames/JPL-Caltech, NASA/SDO; pp 4/5 - European Southern Observatory; pp 6/7 - NASA; pp 8/9 - NASA; pp 10/11 - NASA; pp 12/13 - NASA; pp 14/15 - NASA; pp 16/17 - European Southern Observatory, Francisco Romero; pp 18/19 - NASA; pp 20/21 - Servet Gürbüz, NASA; pp 22/23 - Pgiam; p 36 - NASA.

A CIP catalogue record of this book is available from the British Library.
All rights reserved. No part of this publication may be reproduced, stored in a retrieval system, or transmitted, in any form or by any means, electronic, mechanical, photocopying, recording or otherwise, without the prior permission of the publishers.
The rights of David Orme to be identified as the author and of Dan Chernett to be identified as the illustrator of this Work have been asserted by them in accordance with sections 77 and 78 of the Copyright, Design and Patents Act 1988.

Contents

Planet Hunting: The Facts — 5

1. Our solar system — 6
2. The inner planets — 8
3. The gas giants — 10
4. Exploring the Moon — 12
5. More moons — 14
6. Life – why on Earth? — 16
7. Dwarf planets — 18
8. More planets — 20
9. Radio telescopes — 22

Blast Off to Europa! — 25

Planet Hunting: The Facts

Our solar system

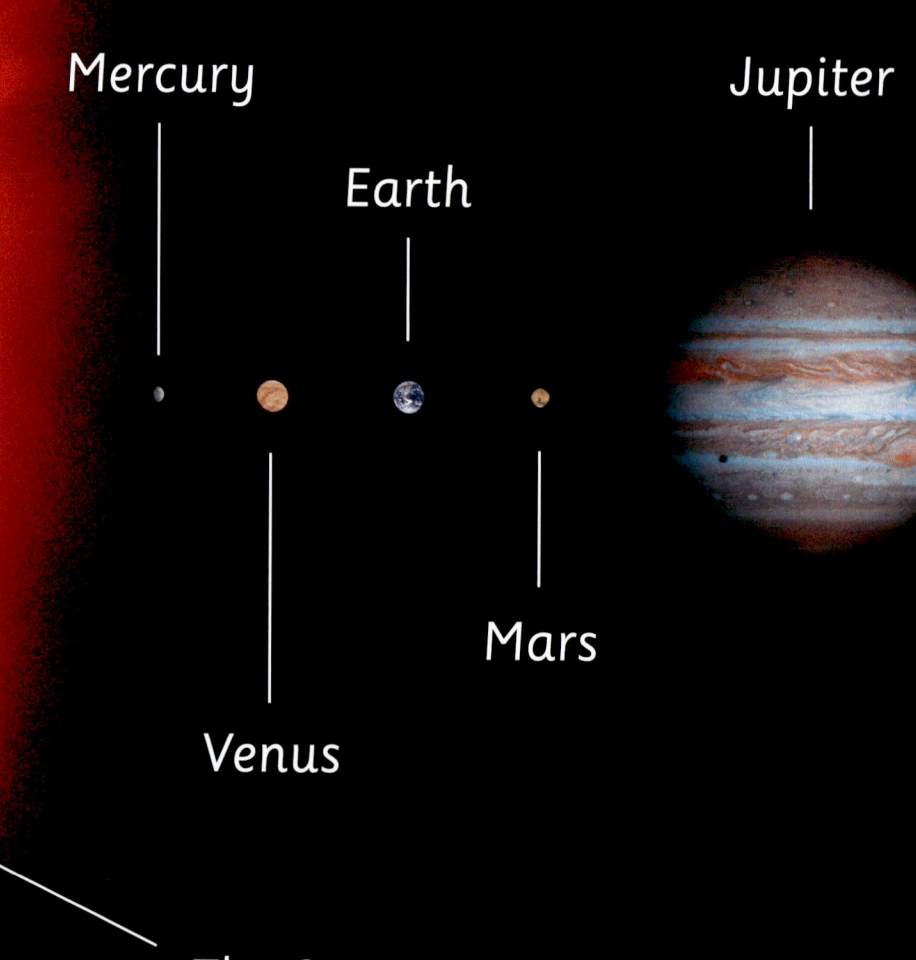

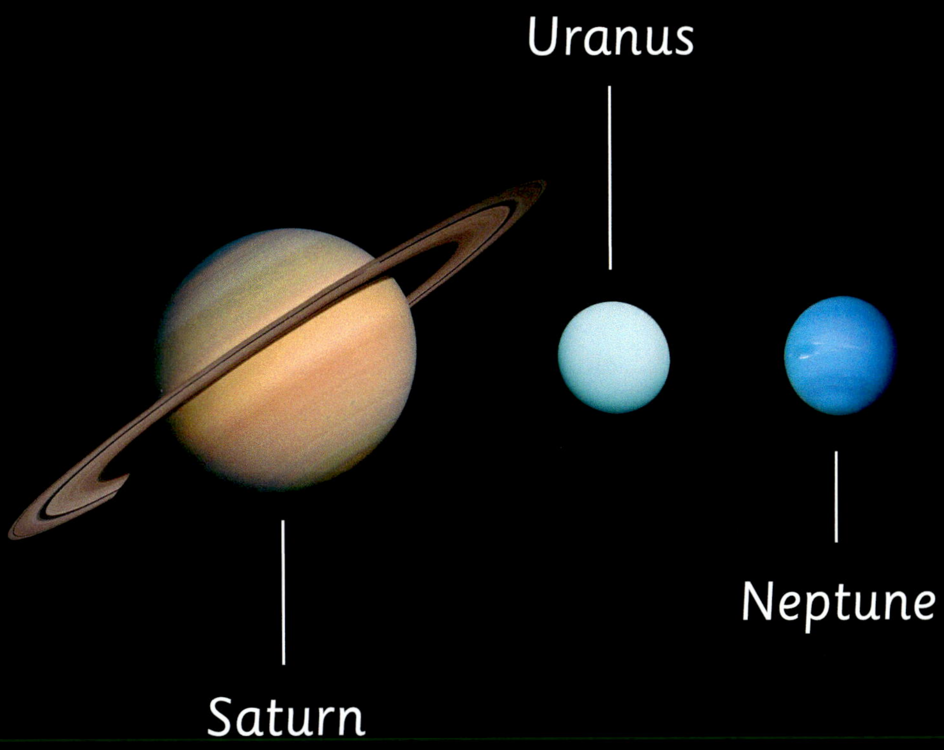

Uranus

Saturn

Neptune

The inner planets

Mercury

How far from the Sun?	58 million km
How long is the day?	59 Earth days
How long is a year?	88 Earth days
How many moons?	None

Venus

How far from the Sun?	108 million km
How long is the day?	224 Earth days
How long is a year?	227 Earth days
How many moons?	None

Earth

How far from the Sun?	150 million km
How long is the day?	24 hours
How long is a year?	365 days
How many moons?	One

Mars

How far from the Sun?	228 million km
How long is the day?	24.5 Earth hours
How long is a year?	687 Earth days
How many moons?	Two

The gas giants

Jupiter – the biggest planet

How far from the Sun?	780 million km
How long is the day?	10 Earth hours
How long is a year?	12 Earth years
How many moons?	At least 66!

Saturn

How far from the Sun?	1,400 million km
How long is the day?	10.5 Earth hours
How long is a year?	30 Earth years
How many moons?	At least 62

Uranus

How far from the Sun?	2,870 million km
How long is the day?	17 Earth hours
How long is a year?	84 Earth years
How many moons?	At least 27

Neptune

How far from the Sun?	4,500 million km
How long is the day?	16 Earth hours
How long is a year?	165 Earth years
How many moons?	At least 13

Exploring the Moon

This is Neil Armstrong. He was the first man to step on the Moon – in 1969.

A footprint on the Moon.

A Moon buggy.

How many Moon landings have there been?

Six. The last one was in 1972.

Will we go back to the Moon?

Yes. We could use the Moon as a base to explore the planets.

More moons

The gas giants have lots of moons. Some of them are as big as a small planet.

This is Titan. It is Saturn's biggest moon. It has a thick atmosphere.

Could there be life on Titan? No. It's too cold.

This is Europa, a moon of Jupiter.

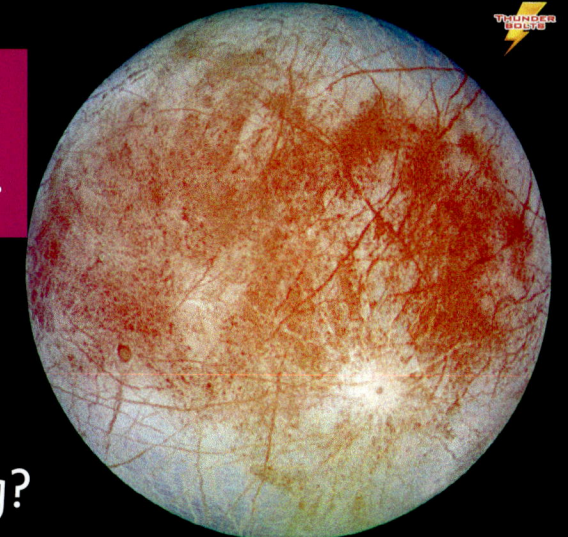

Why is it interesting?

That smooth surface is ice. Some scientists think there is water underneath it. There may be living things there.

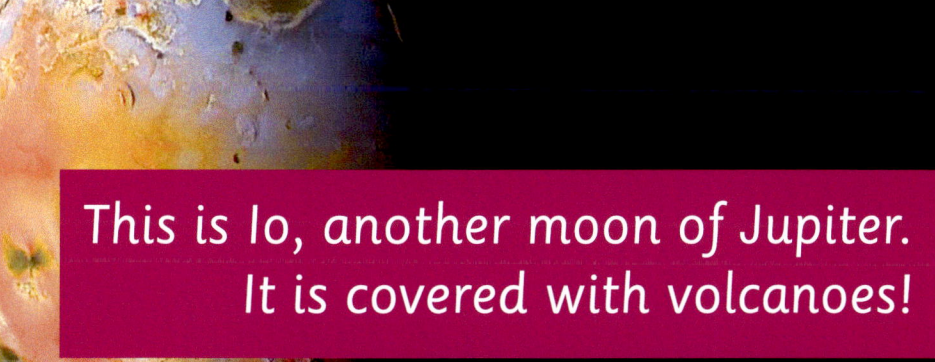

This is Io, another moon of Jupiter. It is covered with volcanoes!

Life – why on Earth?

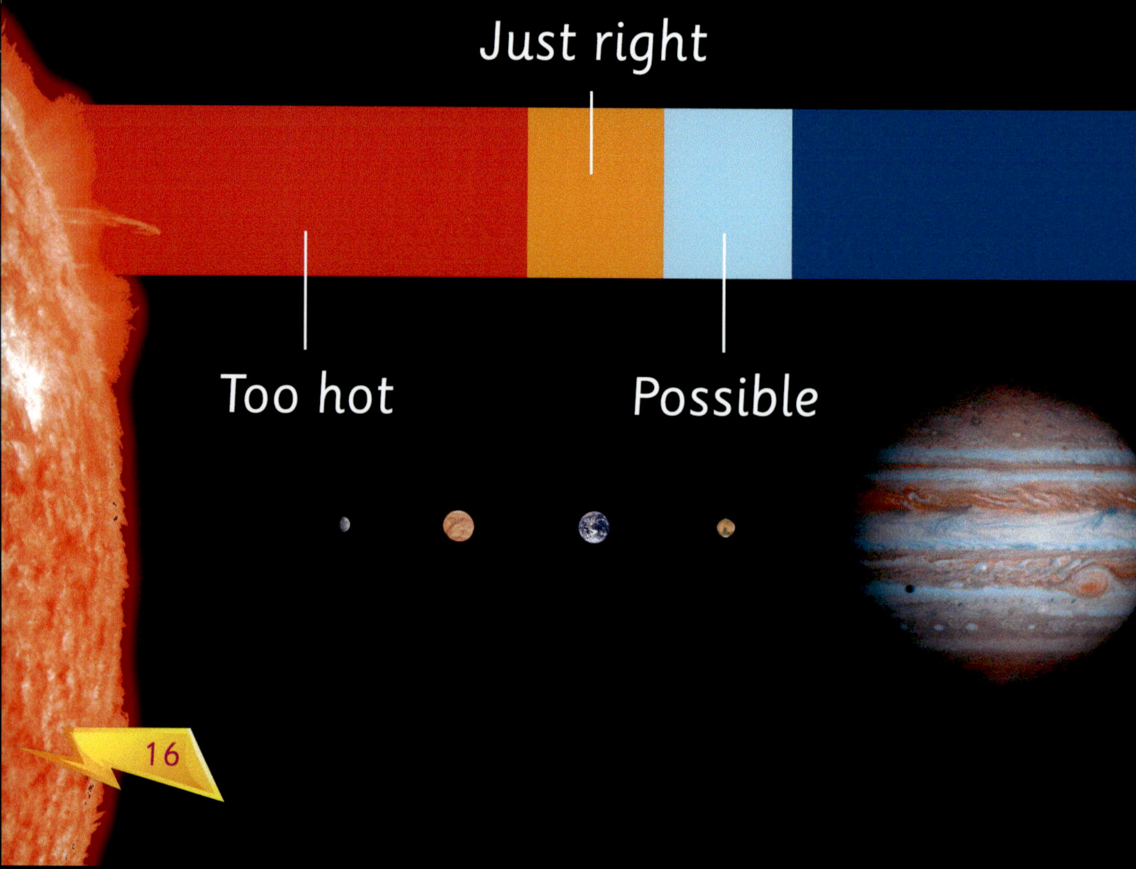

Just right

Too hot

Possible

Too cold

Dwarf planets

What is a dwarf planet?

1. It goes round the Sun.
2. It is much smaller than other planets.

Pluto – a dwarf planet.

Eris – a dwarf planet as big as Pluto. It is 14.5 billion km from the Sun!

How many dwarf planets are there?

We just don't know!

More planets

Where can we find more planets?

Around other suns!

Really?

Yes. Lots have been found.

How?

A planet goes in front of the sun …

Radio telescopes

How can we talk to people on other planets?

We can send a message with one of these!

Any problems?

Yes. It would take many years to get an answer!

Blast Off to Europa!

One year later ...

Nearly there!

But she does it anyway ...

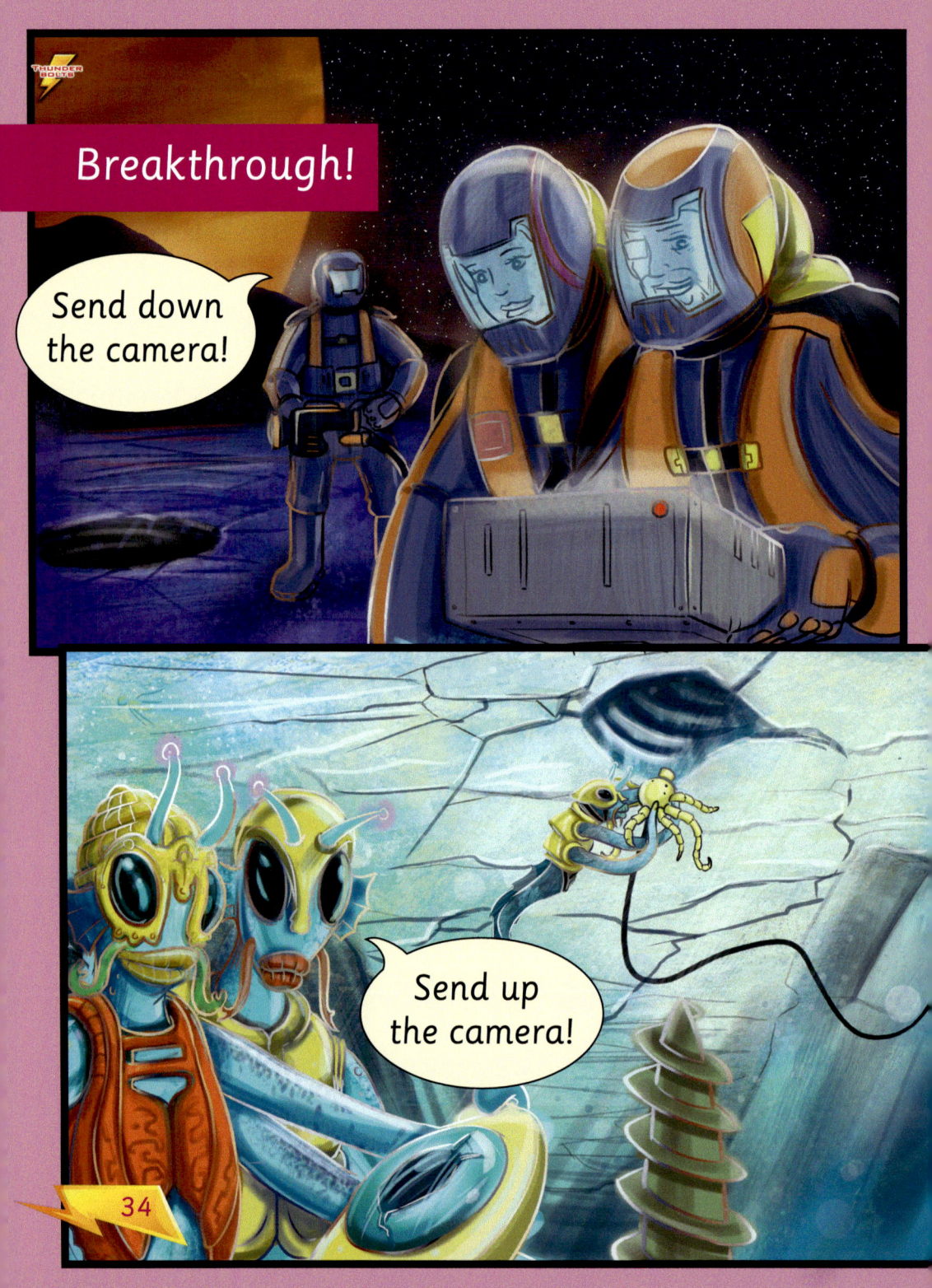

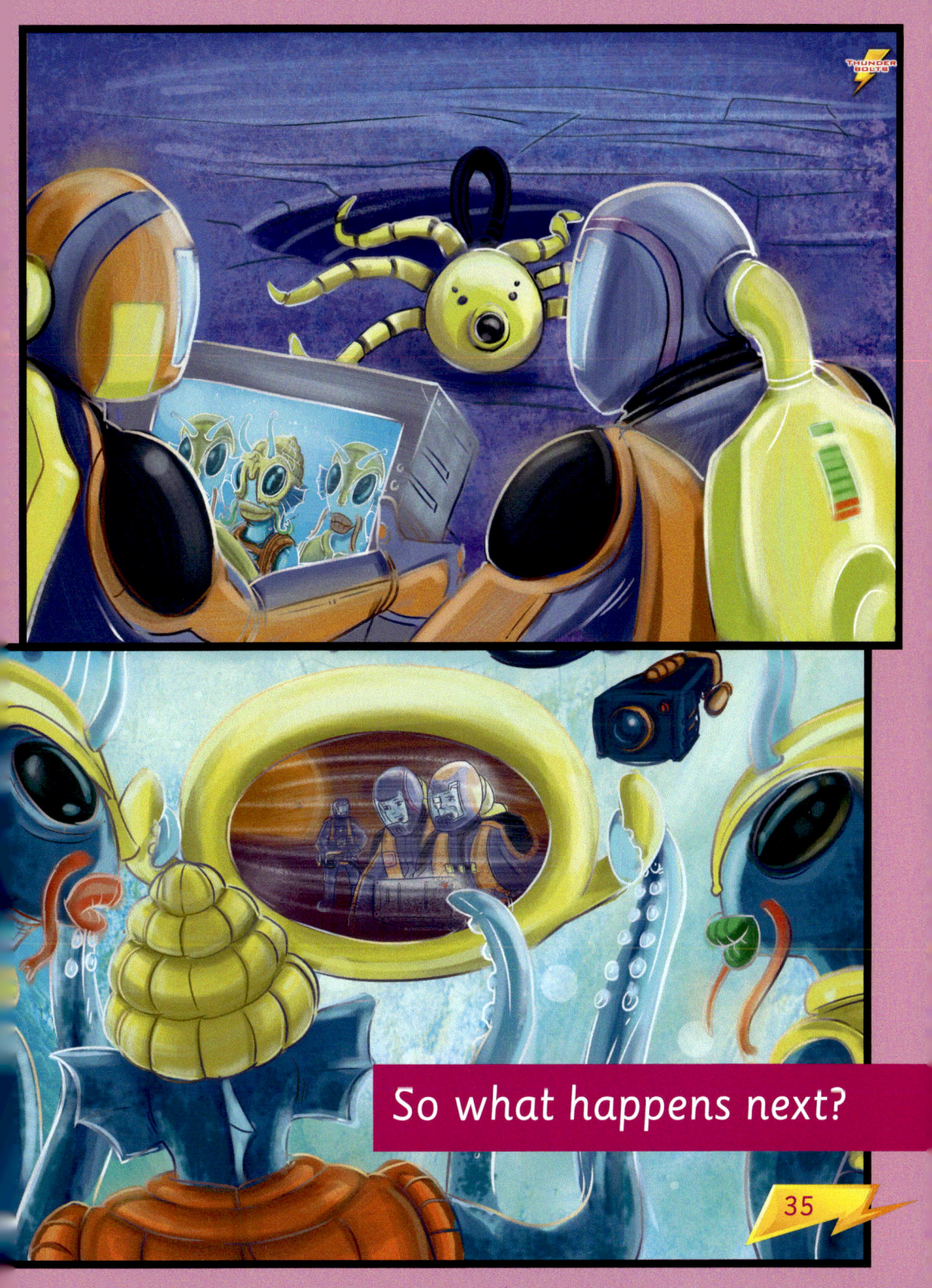

Word list

dwarf planet
Earth
Eris
Europa
gas giant
Io
Jupiter
Mars
Mercury
moon
Moon buggy

Neptune
planet
Pluto
radio telescope
Saturn
solar system
sun
Titan
Uranus
Venus